WHO WOULD WIN?

KILLER WHALE

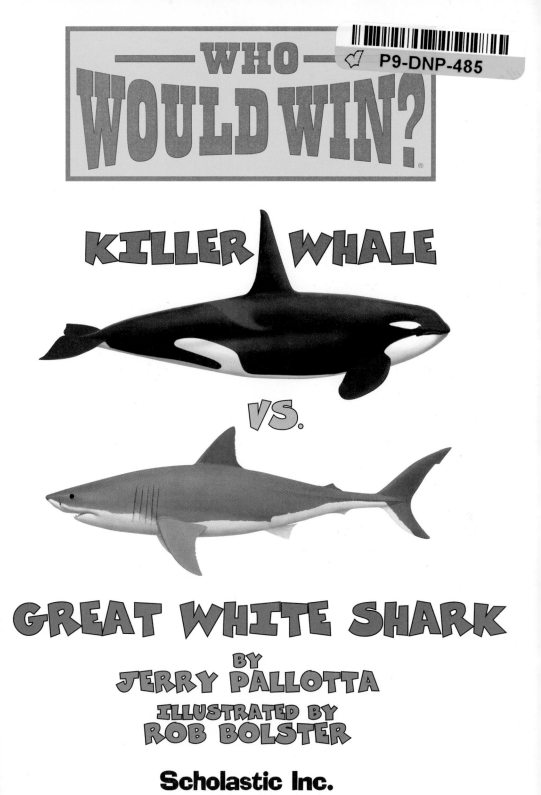

VS.

GREAT WHITE SHARK

BY
JERRY PALLOTTA

ILLUSTRATED BY
ROB BOLSTER

Scholastic Inc.

New York   Toronto   London   Auckland
Sydney   Mexico City   New Delhi   Hong Kong

The publisher would like to thank the following for their
kind permission to use their photographs in this book:

page 6: © Skulls Unlimited; page 7: © Seapics.com; page 12: © pbpgalleries / Alamy;
page 13: © geckophoto / iStockphoto; page 14: © Brandon Cole; page 15: © J. L. & Hubert M. L. Klein /
Biosphoto / Peter Arnold Inc.; page 20: © Alaska Stock LLC / Alamy; page 21: © Brandon Cole

Thank you to my research assistants, Olivia Packenham and Will Harney.
—J.P.

ISBN 978-0-545-16075-9

40 39 38 37 36 35 34 33 32 31   15/0

Printed in the U.S.A.   40
First printing, September 2009

What would happen if a killer whale met up with a great white shark? What if they had a fight? Who do you think would win?

Meet the killer whale, also known as an orca. It is a sea mammal. It breathes air through the blowhole on the top o its head. Just like you, killer whales have lungs. They hold their breath underwater.

← BLOWHOLE →

KILLER WHALE NICKNAMES:
BLACKFISH, ORCA, SEAWOLF,
and
KILLER OF WHALES

Meet the great white shark. It's a huge fish that can't survive out of the water. Sharks and other fish don't breathe air. Fish get oxygen from water that flows through their gills.

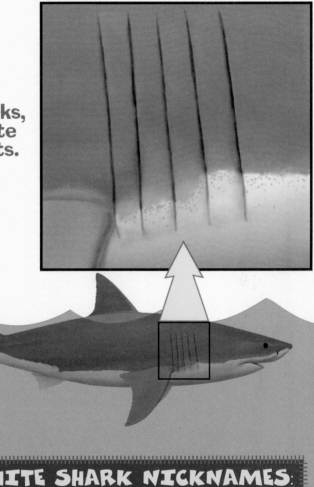

Like most sharks, the great white has five gill slits.

GREAT WHITE SHARK NICKNAMES:
MAN-EATER, TOMMY, WHITE POINTER, and *WHITE DEATH*

The killer whale has a huge jaw full of about fifty teeth. The teeth can be almost four inches long.

Gum line

DID YOU KNOW?

If the killer whale loses an adult tooth, it doesn't grow back.

ACTUAL SIZE

A killer whale tooth looks like this!

A great white shark has a gigantic mouth full of several rows of razor-sharp teeth. It's scary just to look at them.

DID YOU KNOW?

If a shark loses a tooth, another tooth takes its place. During a shark's life, it can lose more than 3,000 teeth.

ACTUAL SIZE

A great white shark tooth looks like this!

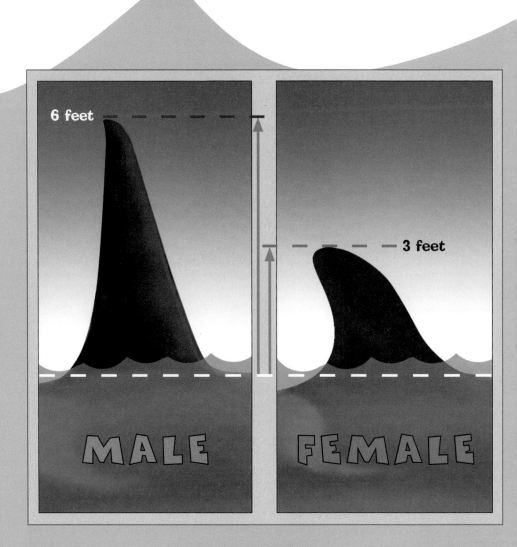

The killer whale's dorsal fin looks like these. On a male killer whale, the dorsal fin can be up to six feet tall.

Killer whales can be found in all oceans.

Male and female great white sharks have dorsal fins that look the same.

Great white sharks are also found in all oceans.

Killer whales are meat eaters. Their favorite foods are seals and sea lions, but they also eat salmon and other fish. A killer whale was once seen grabbing a moose and a deer off the shoreline!

The killer whale is king of the food chain. It has no natural enemies.

The ocean is more like a food __web__ than a food chain. In the ocean, everything eats almost everything else.

Great white sharks eat fish,
but have also been known to eat
seals, sea lions, and even sea turtles.
Now and then, they eat a few people.

A great white shark is also high on the
food chain. It is the largest predatory fish.

*Tiny plankton is eaten
by small fish. Small fish get eaten by
bigger fish. Bigger fish get eaten
by larger fish, and so on.*

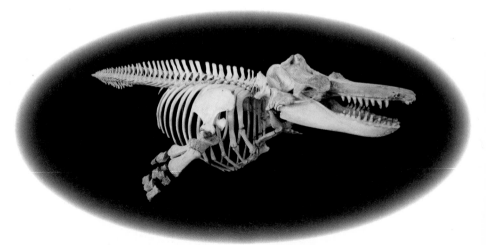

MALE

23 feet

19 feet

FEMALE

A male killer whale is bigger than a female killer whale. A female is about four feet shorter.

Killer whales have bones. This is a killer whale skeleton.

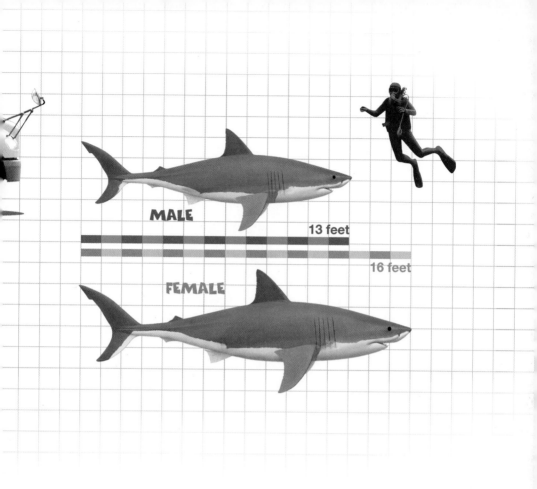

MALE

13 feet

16 feet

FEMALE

The female great white shark is bigger than the male. Females are wider and about three feet longer.

LOOK! NO BONES!

Great white sharks do not have bones. Shark skeletons are made of cartilage. Feel your own ear. It is made of cartilage.

Although they are huge, killer whales can jump completely out of the water.

DID YOU KNOW?

Killer whales might jump for fun, to knock some whale lice off their skin, or to catch a fish or a seal.

In a fight, who do you think would win? A killer whale or a great white shark?

DID YOU KNOW?
Great white
sharks have been
seen leaping into the
air to catch a seal
or a sea lion.

Wow! Great white sharks can jump completely out of the water too!

So look at the facts! Who do you think has an advantage? Who would win?

Like other sea mammals, killer whales have a horizontal tail.

Like other sharks, a great white shark
has a vertical tail.

SONAR

Killer whales have no ears. They bounce sounds off of approaching fish. They use sonar to navigate, to locate other creatures in the ocean, and to find each other. They recognize echoes and other vibrations in the water. This is called echolocation.

Bonus Fact!

SONAR
is an acronym:
SOund
Navigation
And
Ranging

DID YOU KNOW?
Submarines also use sonar, but nature had it first. Bats use sonar too!

Underwater, you look like this t a killer whale.

SMELL

Underwater, the great white shark senses your electricity.

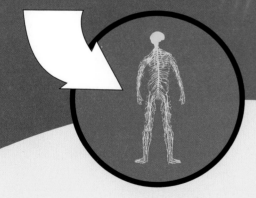

Great white sharks have a keen sense of smell. They can also detect the electricity in fish and other animals. They can tell if you are nervous.

Killer whales are family oriented. They live in groups called pods. Killer whale moms, dads, aunts, uncles, cousins, and kids eat, swim, and play together. They look out for each other.

Great white sharks are loners. Two and three have been seen hunting as a team. But mostly they travel,

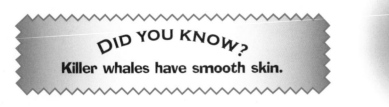

Killer whales can stop swimming and tread water in one place. They can swim up to thirty miles per hour. In the ocean, that is fast!

DID YOU KNOW?
Killer whales have smooth skin.

SPEED LIMIT 30

SPEED
LIMIT
20

Great white sharks never stop swimming. Seawater must flow through their gills so they can get oxygen. They cruise along at about two miles per hour, but speed up in bursts to twenty miles per hour.

Bonus Fact!

Great white sharks have rough skin. It is like sandpaper. Most fish have scales. Sharks have denticles. Denticles are like little tiny teeth on their skin.

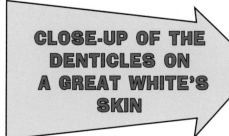

CLOSE-UP OF THE DENTICLES ON A GREAT WHITE'S SKIN

Killer Whale Brain

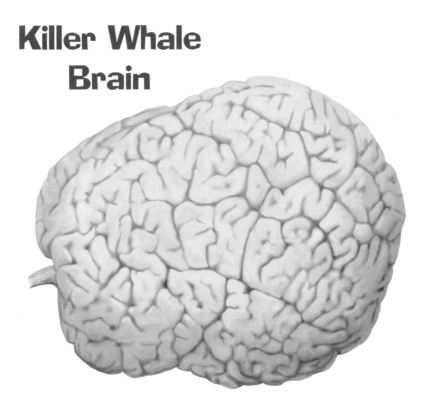

A killer whale's brain looks similar to a human brain, but is three times larger. Killer whales are extremely intelligent.

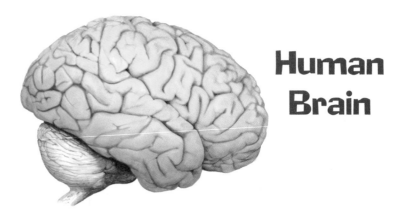

Human Brain

Great White Shark Brain

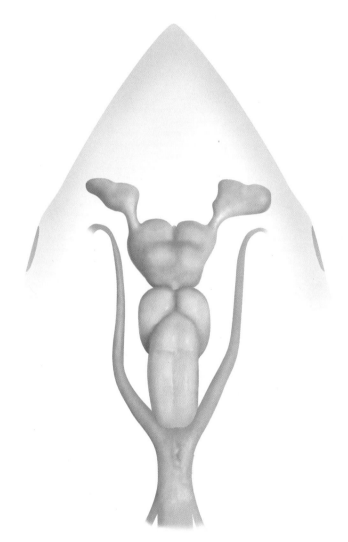

A great white shark does not have a round brain. It has different sections connected together. It is shaped like a letter "Y." Scientists think every section is connected to a different sense.

A killer whale can be captured, live in captivity, and trained to perform tricks. Killer whales are stars at aquariums and amusement parks.

Great white sharks have never been able to survive long in captivity. Hollywood loves to make movies about them. Great white sharks are movie stars!

WHO WOULD WIN?

now playing

KILLER WHALE
VS.
GREAT WHITE SHARK

FUN FACT:
Jaws *is one of the most popular movies of all time. For years, moviegoers were afraid to swim at the beach. Everyone knows the music: Dun! Dun! Dun! Dun! Dun! Dun!*

So, what would happen if a killer whale and a great white shark met in the ocean?

What if they were the same size?
What if they were both hungry?
What if they had a fight?

Uh-oh! They are in the same place at the same time!
They sense each other. There is intense competition in
nature. They are each planning their attacks!

Great white sharks like to attack from below.
Killer whales like to attack from any side.
They are getting closer. Then the fight happens.

CRUNCH!

The great white shark makes the first move. It tries to attack with its sharp teeth. The killer whale outsmarts the shark and bites it. One! Two! Three seconds! The fight is over! It is no contest! The ferocious great white shark doesn't know what hit it.

The killer whale won today. What do you think will happen the next time a killer whale meets a great white shark? Who would win? Do you think the shark can overcome a killer whale's superior intelligence?

KILLER WHALE

GREAT WHITE SHARK

☐	Breathing	☐
☐	Teeth	☐
☐	Dorsal fin	☐
☐	Size	☐
☐	Tail	☐
☐	Smell	☐
☐	Vision	☐
☐	Family	☐
☐	Intelligence	☐
☐	Speed	☐